Things to Know When Selecting a Payment Gateway

First published by Kjøller 2023

Table of Contents

Introduction

In today's digital age, running an online business is practically impossible without a reliable payment gateway. But with so many options available, choosing the right one for your business can be an overwhelming task. From transaction fees and security measures to integration and customer support, there are numerous factors to consider before making a decision. That's where this book comes in - providing you with essential information and insights, so you can make an informed decision when selecting a payment gateway. Whether you're just starting out or are an established business, this book will help you navigate the complex world of payment gateways and find the best fit for your needs.

Acceptable Use Policy

a set of guidelines and restrictions implemented by payment gateways to ensure merchants are not engaging in illegal or unethical business practices.

Acquiring Bank

a financial institution that processes payments on behalf of merchants and is responsible for depositing funds into a merchant's designated account.

American Express SafeKey

a 3D Secure authentication feature specific to American Express cardholders, offering an additional layer of security during online transactions.

Anti-fraud tools

security measures implemented by payment gateways to protect merchants and customers from fraudulent transactions, such as card verification and fraud detection algorithms.

API

a set of programming instructions that allow software to interact with other software, in this case allowing communication between a website's shopping cart and the payment gateway.

API Access Token

a unique code provided to merchants by the payment gateway that allows them to securely access and transmit transactional data.

API Integration

Payment gateway APIs enable merchants to integrate the payment gateway into their website or mobile app seamlessly. The API documentation and ease of integration are essential factors to consider when selecting a payment gateway.

Authentication

the process of verifying a customer's identity before allowing them to complete a transaction, often with personal information or a secure login.

Authorization

the process of verifying that a customer has the necessary funds or credit available for a transaction.

Automatic recurring billing

a feature that allows merchants to automatically charge customers on a regular basis, often used for subscription-based businesses.

AVS (Address Verification System)

a fraud prevention measure that compares the numerical portion of a customer's address provided during checkout with the billing address on file with their financial institution.

Bank Identification Number (BIN)

The first six digits of a credit card number that identifies the issuing bank of the card. Payment gateways use this information to validate the card and ensure that it is not fraudulent.

Bank Transfer

A payment method that allows customers to transfer funds directly from their bank account to the merchant's account. This is typically slower than credit card payments, but may be preferred by customers who do not have a credit card or do not want to use one for online purchases.

Batch Processing

A feature provided by payment gateways that allows merchants to process multiple transactions at once. This is useful for merchants who receive large volumes of transactions on a daily basis.

Billing Address

The physical address associated with the credit card or other payment method being used for the transaction. This is required by the payment gateway to verify the transaction and prevent fraud.

Billing Descriptor

The description of a transaction that appears on a customer's billing statement. This should be clear and concise to avoid confusion and prevent chargebacks.

BIN Database

A database of credit card BINs that is used by payment gateways to validate credit card transactions and prevent fraud. These databases are maintained by third-party providers and are updated regularly.

Braintree

An online payment gateway owned by PayPal that allows merchants to accept payments from customers using credit cards, PayPal, and other payment methods.

Business Account

An account provided by a payment gateway that is designed specifically for merchants who need to accept payments online. This account provides access to additional features such as fraud detection and chargeback management.

Buyer Authentication

The process of verifying the identity of a buyer during a payment transaction. This involves the use of a two-factor authentication process, such as a password and OTP, to ensure that only the authorized user can complete the payment.

Buyer Protection

A feature provided by some payment gateways that helps protect buyers from fraud and unauthorized transactions. This may include things like chargeback protection and dispute resolution services.

Card Saving

Payment gateways may save the customer's card details for future transactions, and merchants must ensure that this is compliant with relevant regulations and standards. Merchants should also offer customers the option to opt-out of card saving to enhance their data privacy and security.

Card Types

Payment gateways should accept various card types, such as credit cards, debit cards, and prepaid cards, to cater to a broader customer base.

Chargeback

When a customer disputes a transaction and the funds are reversed back to the customer by the bank or credit card company, this process is called chargeback. A payment gateway with efficient chargeback management is essential as it can impact the merchant's reputation and revenue.

Chargeback Fees

Payment gateways may charge a fee per chargeback, and merchants must be aware of the charges levied by the gateway provider. Comparing chargeback fees can help merchants select the most cost-effective and efficient payment gateway.

Checkout Process

The checkout page is crucial as it determines the customer's experience and conversion rate. The payment gateway should have a seamless checkout process that is easy to use and transparent.

Compliance

Payment gateways must adhere to specific standards and regulations, such as PCI-DSS, to safeguard customer information and ensure secure transactions. Failure to comply with these standards can result in legal actions and reputational damage.

Currency Conversion

Payment gateways must support a wide range of currencies to streamline international transactions. They should also offer competitive exchange rates without additional fees for currency conversion.

Customer Support

In case of issues or queries, merchants should have access to efficient customer support services, such as phone, email, or live chat. A responsive support team enhances the merchant's trust and confidence in the payment gateway provider.

Customization

Merchants should have the flexibility to customize the payment gateway to match their branding and website design. Customization options may include adding logos, themes, and colors to enhance the user's overall experience.

Data Encryption

The process of converting sensitive data into an unreadable format to prevent unauthorized access. Payment gateways use sophisticated encryption techniques to ensure secure transmission of credit card information.

Decline Codes

A decline code is a numerical code assigned by a payment gateway that corresponds to a specific reason for a declined transaction. Understanding these codes can help merchants identify and resolve issues with their payment gateway to avoid future declines.

Delayed Capture

Delayed capture is a feature offered by some payment gateways that allows merchants to authorize a transaction at the time of purchase, but only capture the funds at a later time. This can be useful for merchants who need to verify the availability of a product before capturing payment.

Digital Signature

A digital signature is a unique identifier used to authenticate the integrity of electronic documents, such as contracts or receipts. Payment gateways may require digital signatures as an additional layer of security for certain types of transactions.

Digital Wallet

A digital wallet is a virtual version of a physical wallet used to store payment information for online transactions. Payment gateways can be integrated with popular digital wallets to offer quicker and easier checkout experiences for customers.

Direct Debit

A payment method that allows merchants to automatically withdraw funds from a customer's bank account. Direct debit payments can be processed through some payment gateways, depending on the gateway's capabilities.

Dispute Management

The process of managing and resolving chargebacks or disputes related to fraudulent or unauthorized transactions. Payment gateways often offer dispute management services to help merchants handle these issues efficiently.

Dual Interface

A type of payment card that contains both contact and contactless interfaces, allowing for more flexible payment options. Payment gateways must be able to process both contact and contactless transactions for cards with dual interfaces.

Dynamic Authentication

A method of authentication used by some payment gateways that involves the use of dynamic data, such as biometric information, to verify the identity of the user. Dynamic authentication can provide an additional layer of security for high-risk transactions.

Dynamic Currency Conversion

A feature offered by some payment gateways that allows customers to pay for goods or services in their own currency, with the conversion handled by the payment gateway.

E-commerce

E-commerce is a business model that involves buying and selling products and services online. Payment Gateways play a crucial role in facilitating e-commerce transactions by providing secure payment processing services to online merchants.

EMV Compliance

EMV compliance refers to the standard set by Europay, Mastercard, and Visa for secure payment processing using chip-enabled credit and debit cards. Payment Gateways that are EMV compliant provide additional security against card fraud, making online transactions more secure.

Encryption

Encryption refers to the process of converting sensitive information into a code to protect it from unauthorized access. Payment Gateways use encryption to securely transmit the sensitive data from the customer's device to the merchant's server. TLS, SSL, and 3D secure are some common encryption methods used by Payment Gateways.

Error Handling

Error handling refers to the process of detecting, diagnosing, and resolving errors that occur during the payment processing cycle. Payment Gateways should have robust error handling capabilities to prevent transaction failures and ensure smooth payment processing.

Escrow Services

Escrow services refer to the intermediary service provided by Payment Gateways to hold funds in a secure account until the transaction is completed successfully. Escrow services are commonly used for high-value transactions, where the risk of fraud or dispute is high.

Expiration Date

The expiration date is the date on the card or account when the cardholder's authorization to use the card or account expires. It is an essential piece of information collected during the payment process by Payment Gateways to ensure that the customer has provided a valid payment method.

Express Checkout

Express Checkout refers to the streamlined checkout process provided by some Payment Gateways to reduce the time and effort required to complete a transaction. It typically involves a one-click checkout process that allows users to complete transactions quickly without entering any additional information.

Facilitator

This is the entity that enables the payment transaction between the buyer and the seller. It can be a payment gateway or a payment processor in most cases. In some payment gateway models, the payment facilitator is responsible for handling the entire payment process, from authorization to settlement, while in others, the payment facilitator is just a part of the process.

Fast Checkout

A fast checkout system allows for quick payments without requiring the buyer to type in their payment and shipping information for every transaction. It saves time for customers and helps improve the conversion rate of a platform. Many payment gateways offer a fast checkout option such as PayPal OneTouch, Apple Pay, Google Pay, and others.

Fees

Payment gateways charge different fees in different ways. They may charge a setup fee, transaction fee, monthly fee, or a combination of them. There can also be additional fees for chargebacks, refunds, international transactions, and others. It is important to understand the fee structure and compare it with other payment gateways to choose the most affordable one.

Financial Institution

This is the bank that holds the account of the merchant or the buyer. Payment gateways work with different financial institutions that process the transactions and handle the settlement process. It is important to choose a trusted financial institution that can provide secure and reliable services.

Foreign Exchange (FX) Fees

These fees occur when a transaction is processed in a currency different from the native currency of the bank account. Some payment gateways offer FX conversion as an additional service, and they charge a fee for it. It is important to know the FX fees to determine the overall cost of a transaction.

Fraud Management Systems

These are systems that help identify fraudulent activities during a transaction. They use different techniques to detect fraudulent activities such as analyzing transaction patterns, device fingerprinting, IP geolocation, and behavioral analysis. Some payment gateways offer built-in fraud management systems, while others integrate with third-party providers.

Fraud Prevention Tools

These are tools that help prevent fraudulent activities before they occur. They can include address verification, CVV verification, risk scoring, and 3-D secure. These tools help minimize the risk of chargebacks and enhance the overall security of a platform.

Fraud Score

This is a score assigned to a transaction that indicates the likelihood of fraudulent activity. Payment gateways use various criteria to calculate the fraud score, including the cardholder's address, IP location, previous chargebacks, and the transaction amount. By analyzing the fraud score, payment gateways can trigger different actions such as requiring additional verification or declining the transaction altogether.

Friendly Fraud

This is a term used to describe chargeback fraud, where a buyer disputes a transaction that they actually made. It often happens when the buyer forgets they made the purchase or wants to avoid the cost of returning the product. Payment gateways with advanced fraud prevention tools can help reduce friendly fraud cases.

Funding Sources

These are the sources used to fund a transaction. Payment gateways can process transactions from different funding sources, such as credit cards, bank transfers, PayPal, Bitcoin, and others. It is important to select a payment gateway that supports the most suitable funding source for the target audience of a platform.

Gateway

A gateway is a platform that connects buyers, sellers, and banks to process transactions. A payment gateway is responsible for securely transmitting transaction data between the customer and the merchant. It is the front-end piece of a payment processing system.

Gateway Dashboard

A gateway dashboard is a web-based interface that provides merchants with access to their transaction data, reports, and account settings. Merchants can use the gateway dashboard to monitor transaction activity, track payments, and customize their payment processing settings.

Gateway Fees

Gateway fees are the costs associated with using a payment gateway's services. These fees can include transaction fees, monthly fees, setup fees, and chargeback fees. Merchants need to consider the gateway fees when selecting a payment gateway that aligns with their business needs and budget.

Gateway Integration

Gateway integration refers to the process of connecting an online store's shopping cart to a payment gateway. Payment gateways offer various integration options, including API, hosted pages, and plugins. Merchants can choose the integration option that aligns with their technical capabilities and website platform.

Gateway Provider

A gateway provider is the company that provides the payment gateway service. Merchants choose a gateway provider based on their specific business requirements, such as transaction volume, accepted payment methods, and technical capabilities. Gateway providers charge gateway fees for their services.

Gateway Security

Gateway security refers to the measures taken by a payment gateway to ensure that customer information and transaction data are safe and secure. Payment gateways use various security protocols, such as SSL encryption, fraud detection, and PCI compliance, to prevent data breaches and protect against fraud.

Gateway Tokenization

Gateway tokenization is the process of replacing sensitive customer data, such as card numbers, with a unique identifier called a token. Tokenization improves payment security by reducing the risk of data breaches and protecting customer information. Payment gateways use tokenization to store customer data securely and process repeat transactions.

Geolocation

Geolocation is the process of identifying and locating the physical location of a device or user. Payment gateways use geolocation technology to verify the customer's location and prevent fraudulent transactions. Geolocation is used to match the IP address and the location of the cardholder's billing address.

Global Payment Methods

Global payment methods refer to the payment options that are widely accepted around the world. Payment gateways need to support global payment methods for merchants to offer a seamless checkout experience to customers in different countries. These payment methods include credit and debit cards, digital wallets, and bank transfers.

Hashing

A method used to encrypt sensitive data during transit, such as credit card information. Hashing ensures the security of data and prevents it from being intercepted or stolen by hackers.

Header

The top section of a Payment Gateway page that typically includes the merchant's logo, branding, and other important information such as the total amount due, and the checkout process steps.

Helpdesk

A support team that is available to assist merchants with technical issues with their Payment Gateway, such as integration, configuration, and troubleshooting.

High Risk

Payment Gateway providers have systems in place to detect high-risk transactions, such as those involving large sums of money, international payments, or those with a high incidence of fraud. Merchants operating in so-called "high-risk" industries may need to pay higher processing rates.

Holdback

A portion of funds held back by a Payment Gateway provider as a reserve against chargebacks and other losses in case of fraudulent transactions. Holdbacks can range from a percentage of each transaction to a fixed amount of funds held in reserve.

Hosted Checkout

A Payment Gateway checkout page that is hosted on the provider's website, rather than on the merchant's website. This can reduce legal and compliance risks for the merchant, as the provider is responsible for handling sensitive data.

Hosted Payment Pages

Similar to hosted checkout pages, hosted payment pages are a secure and PCI-compliant way to accept payments online, but the checkout pages are hosted on the Payment Gateway provider's website rather than the merchant's. Hosted payment pages are typically used by small businesses that want to get up and running quickly with an online store without investing in extensive technical infrastructure or expertise.

Hosting

The physical location in which the Payment Gateway software resides, and where data is stored for processing. Hosting can be done either by the Payment Gateway provider or by a third-party vendor.

HSM (Hardware Security Module)

A hardware-based encryption and decryption device that is used to protect sensitive data and ensure the security of transactions processed through a Payment Gateway.

HTML

The code used to create and design the user interface and checkout pages on a Payment Gateway. Merchants can customize their HTML code to create a webstore that matches their brand and business needs.

Inactivity fees

Fees charged by a payment gateway for accounts that remain inactive or underutilized for a prolonged period. Merchants must be aware of the payment gateway's inactivity fee policies to avoid unwanted fees.

In-person transactions

Some payment gateways allow merchants to accept payments in person through a point-of-sale (POS) or card reader device. This type of payment gateway is ideal for businesses that operate physical storefronts, exhibitions or events where buyers can make payments using their debit or credit cards.

Instant settlement

A type of payment gateway that allows merchants to receive payment funds instantly after a transaction is processed. This type of payment gateway is ideal for businesses that rely on quick cash flow for operations or those that experience frequent cash flow variability.

Integration

The process of connecting a payment gateway to an eCommerce website or online store. Integration can be done through APIs or plugins, and it allows the payment gateway to receive payment requests from the website, process them and transfer the payment to the merchant. Good integration is a must-have for seamless transactions and reduces the risk of payment errors.

Integration complexity

The extent of the integration process could range from copy-pasting a few lines of code to a highly complex, multi-step process. The level of time, effort and expertise required to integrate a payment gateway depends on the preferred gateway, platform and other factors such as features and customization.

Integration support

Payment gateway providers often offer integration support to merchants who require technical assistance during the integration process. Integration support can be in the form of comprehensive guides, forums, or direct technical support to troubleshoot code-related or platform-related issues.

Interchange fees

Fees charged by credit card companies to payment gateways for processing transactions. These fees vary by card type and region and are paid by the payment gateway to the credit card company. The payment gateway, in turn, may pass along the cost of the interchange fees to merchants through transaction fees.

International payments

Payment gateways that offer international payment support allow buyers and sellers to process payment transactions in different currencies without incurring currency conversion costs. Merchants must be aware of the fees charged by payment gateways for international payments to avoid unexpected charges.

Invoicing

Invoicing is defined as the process of requesting payment for goods or services rendered through the sending of an invoice. Many payment gateways offer invoicing features allowing merchants to create and send invoices directly through the payment gateway.

Issuing bank

The bank that issues credit or debit cards to buyers. Payment gateways must have a relationship with an issuing bank to process transactions made through credit or debit cards. The issuing bank is responsible for authorizing card transactions on behalf of the buyer and paying the merchant for the transaction amount.

Java

A programming language commonly used in payment gateway development. When selecting a payment gateway provider, it is important to ensure that they use a secure Java-based platform to ensure safe and reliable payment processing.

JavaScript

A popular scripting language used in web development that is often used in payment gateway integration. When selecting a payment gateway provider, it is important to ensure that they support JavaScript integration to ensure smooth and responsive checkout experiences for your customers.

Javelin Strategy & Research

A research and consulting firm specializing in the financial services industry. When selecting a payment gateway, it may be helpful to consult Javelin Strategy & Research for insights and analysis on the latest payment technologies and trends.

JCB

A credit card brand originating from Japan that is widely accepted in Asian countries but not as widely accepted in other parts of the world. When selecting a payment gateway, it is important to ensure that JCB is supported if you want to offer this payment option to your customers in Asia.

JCB International Co., Ltd.

A subsidiary of JCB that provides payment gateway services to merchants around the world. When selecting a payment gateway, it is important to consider JCB International Co., Ltd. as a potential provider if you want to offer JCB payment options to your customers.

J-curve

A graph that illustrates the short-term increase in costs or loss before eventual long-term gains or profits. In the context of payment gateways, it may be necessary to invest in initial setup costs or pay transaction fees before ultimately seeing long-term benefits in increased sales and customer satisfaction.

Joint Liability

A legal concept that holds multiple parties responsible for a debt or obligation. In the context of payment gateways, this means that both the merchant and the payment gateway provider can be held liable for any fraud or payment disputes that may arise. It is important to understand the joint liability terms and conditions when selecting a payment gateway to ensure that both parties are protected.

JPay

A payment processing company specializing in providing payment solutions for correctional facilities and families of inmates. When selecting a payment gateway, it is important to consider JPay as a potential provider if your business operates in the corrections industry.

JSON

A lightweight data interchange format used in web services and APIs. When selecting a payment gateway provider, it is important to ensure that they support JSON integration to ensure efficient and seamless data exchange.

Jurisdiction

The geographical area where a legal authority has the power to make and enforce laws. When selecting a payment gateway, it is important to ensure that the provider operates in a jurisdiction that aligns with your business needs and legal requirements.

Keyed Entry

Keyed entry is the practice of manually entering a credit or debit card number into the payment gateway. Merchants typically use keyed entry when the card is not physically present or when there is a problem with the card's magnetic strip. Keyed entry is typically more expensive than swiping and carries a higher risk of fraud.

Keypad

The keypad is the input device that connects to a payment gateway. It's used to enter PIN codes, passwords, and other verification codes. The keypad is typically securely encased to protect against fraud, and it's an essential part of modern payment processing.

Keystore

The keystore is an encrypted file used to store payments data. It's used to secure sensitive data such as credit card numbers, ownership data, and transaction data. The keystore is an important part of maintaining the integrity of the payment system and is a vital security measure for payment gateway providers.

Kiosk

A kiosk is a self-service payment terminal. It's an excellent option for retailers who operate in areas where there is limited space, as kiosks take up very little real estate. Kiosks offer a reasonable level of security, and they can accept various payment methods such as cash, debit, and credit cards.

Knockout

A knockout is a feature designed to protect merchants against fraudulent transactions. It works by blocking transactions from high-risk areas or individuals, ensuring that the payment gateway process only legitimate transactions.

KPI (Key Performance Indicator)

KPIs are metrics used to determine the success of a payment gateway. Examples of KPIs include average transaction value, conversion rate, and chargeback rate. Merchants should ensure that the gateway they use has metrics that align with their goals and objectives.

KYB (Know Your Business)

KYB is similar to KYC, but it is used to verify the credentials of a business entity rather than an individual. KYB is important because it ensures that the business is legitimate and can be trusted to receive funds from customers.

KYC (Know Your Customer)

KYC is a process that is mandatory for every merchant to complete before using any payment gateway. The process involves providing extensive documentation for the merchant's business and their identity, preventing money laundering or fraud. KYC is important for both, the merchant and the payment gateway, as it ensures the payment processing company doesn't fall foul of anti-crime or anti-terrorism regulations, and the merchant can use a secure payment processing method.

KYCC (Know Your Customer's Customer)

KYCC is an extension of KYC that is used by payment gateways to verify the identities of the customers of the merchants. KYCC ensures the identity of the customer and removes any uncertainty that a fraudulent transaction occurred.

Late Settlement

Late settlement refers to delayed payment after processing the payment. It is crucial to check payment gateway settlement terms and conditions to avoid any negative impact on cash flow.

Level 1 Payment Gateway

A payment gateway that processes more than six million transactions annually. Level 1 gateways are required to comply with PCI DSS Level 1 requirements. They must also have independent third-party PCI DSS auditing.

Liability Shift

When customers use credit cards for their online purchases, the responsibility of chargebacks shifts from the merchant to the payment gateway. If a merchant has implemented 3D secure, then the liability for fraud will shift from the merchant to the cardholder's bank.

Limitations

Every payment gateway can have different limitations in terms of transaction volume, currencies, and countries. Checking the gateway's limitations is essential to ensure there are no roadblocks to using the gateway.

Live Demo

A demo environment of the payment gateway provided to merchants to test the gateway's usability, features, and reporting. It helps merchants to assess the payment gateway before integrating it into their website or application.

Load Balancing

Payment gateways use multiple servers to manage the high volume of transactions. Load balancing technology is used to distribute the traffic across servers to prevent any server from overloading.

Local Payment Methods

Local payment methods refer to any payment method that is not a credit card. It includes bank transfers, online wallets, prepaid cards, and more. Offering local payment methods may increase sales in specific regions where card usage is not prevalent.

Local Taxation

Each country has its own taxation system, which affects the payment gateway's integration. Merchants must check with their payment gateway provider to ensure that the payment gateway can handle the required taxation system.

Low-Cost Payment Gateway

Payment gateways come in various pricing options, from flat rate transaction fees to percentage-based fees. Low-cost payment gateways generally have lower per-transaction costs and fewer add-ons or features.

Loyalty Programs

Some payment gateways offer loyalty programs that reward merchants for performing transactions via their gateway. The rewards can be in the form of discounts, rewards points, or cashback.

Merchant Account

A bank account specifically for accepting credit card payments. The payment gateway will transfer the funds from the customer's credit card to the merchant account.

Merchant Fees

Fees charged by the payment gateway for processing transactions. These fees can be a fixed amount per transaction or a percentage of the transaction value.

Mobile Optimization

The payment gateway's ability to be used on mobile devices. With the increasing use of mobile devices, it's important for payment gateways to have a mobile-friendly interface.

Monthly Fees

Fees charged by the payment gateway on a monthly basis for using their services. These fees can include account maintenance, customer support, and security features.

Multi-Currency Support

The ability to accept payments in multiple currencies. This is important for businesses that operate in different countries or accept international payments.

Near-Field Communication (NFC)

A communication protocol that allows wireless data transfer between devices that are in close proximity to each other, such as a mobile phone and a card reader. NFC technology is commonly used in contactless payments, where a shopper can simply tap their mobile phone or contactless card to make a payment.

Negative Balance Protection

A feature that prevents a merchant's bank account from going into a negative balance due to chargebacks or refunds. When a transaction results in a negative balance, the Payment Gateway automatically deducts the amount from future transactions until the balance is covered.

Net Payment Gateway

A Payment Gateway service that operates by batching transactions and submitting them to the acquiring bank for settlement. This method is often used by small businesses since it offers lower transaction fees and fewer requirements for compliance with PCI DSS standards.

Network Tokenization

A process by which sensitive payment card data is replaced with a unique identifier or token, which is not reversible back to the original account number. This protects cardholder data against theft and fraud since the token can only be used for one transaction and cannot be used to make additional purchases.

Next-Day Funding

A feature that allows a merchant to receive their funds from processed transactions within one business day. This can be beneficial for businesses with cash flow concerns or those that need to reconcile transactions quickly.

NMI

Network Merchants Inc, a Payment Gateway service provider that offers a wide range of solutions tailored to meet the needs of different businesses, from small start-ups to established enterprises.

Non-Compliance Fees

Fees charged to a merchant if they fail to comply with the Payment Card Industry Data Security Standards (PCI DSS). These fees can be substantial and may also result in fines and restrictive limitations on the merchant's ability to process payments.

Non-Refundable Deposit

A payment taken in advance of a service or product being delivered, which is not refundable if the buyer cancels or fails to complete the transaction. This protects the merchant from potential losses while providing some assurance to the buyer of the seller's commitment to provide the product or service as agreed.

Notification of Payment

A feature that sends a message to a merchant when a payment has been processed successfully. This allows merchants to quickly and confidently process transactions, reducing the risk of fraud and errors.

Omni-Channel

The ability to offer payment processing across multiple channels, such as online, mobile, point-of-sale (POS) devices, and in-app payments. An omni-channel payment gateway enables merchants to offer seamless and convenient payment options to customers across different channels.

Onboarding

The process of getting a merchant or buyer signed up with a payment gateway, including verification of identity and ownership of the business. Onboarding can include several steps such as application forms, background checks, and compliance with regulations before the merchant can start processing payments through the gateway.

On-Demand Settlements

The ability to request settlements from a payment gateway on an as-needed basis. On-demand settlements can provide merchants with greater flexibility and control over their cash flow, enabling them to receive funds quickly and on their own schedule. The payment gateway can also provide features such as automatic reconciliation and reporting to simplify settlement processes.

One-Click Checkout

A checkout process that enables customers to complete a purchase with a single click, without having to enter their payment and shipping details manually. One-click checkout can be enabled through a payment gateway's tokenization feature, where the customer's payment details are securely stored for future purchases.

Online Fraud Prevention

The set of tools, technologies, and processes for identifying and preventing fraudulent transactions in online payments. An online payment gateway can use various fraud prevention features such as fraud scoring, risk analysis, real-time monitoring, and two-factor authentication to reduce the risk of fraud.

Open API

An Application Programming Interface (API) that is publicly available and accessible to developers for integration with other software platforms. Open APIs allow developers to create custom integrations, add-on features, and third-party applications that work with the payment gateway.

Order Management

The set of processes and tools for managing and fulfilling online orders, including payment processing, shipping, and tracking. A payment gateway can integrate with a merchant's order management system to provide automated processes for order tracking, inventory management, and delivery management.

Order-to-Cash

The process flow of a transaction, starting from placing an order to receiving payment. Order-to-cash includes various steps such as pricing, invoicing, payment processing, and reconciliation. A payment gateway can provide an end-to-end order-to-cash solution for merchants, enabling them to manage the entire transaction process from a single platform.

Out-of-the-Box Integration

A pre-built integration between a payment gateway and a specific eCommerce or CMS platform, such as WooCommerce, Shopify, or Magento. Out-of-the-box integrations can save time and effort for merchants who want to start accepting payments quickly without having to build their own custom integrations.

Own Branding

The ability to customize the user interface of a payment gateway to match a merchant's own branding, such as logo, colors, and fonts. Own branding can create a seamless and consistent user experience for customers, strengthening the merchant's brand identity.

Payment Authorization

Payment authorization is the process of verifying that a payment card has sufficient funds to cover a requested payment. This involves sending a request to the payment card issuer to confirm that the payment is authorized.

Payment Card Industry (PCI)

The Payment Card Industry (PCI) is an organization that sets and enforces standards for payment card transactions. It is made up of major credit card companies, including Visa, Mastercard, American Express, and Discover.

Payment Fraud

Payment fraud is any fraudulent activity that is carried out during the payment process, including the use of stolen payment card details or the submission of false payment information. It is the responsibility of payment gateways and processors to implement measures to prevent and detect payment fraud.

Payment Gateway

A payment gateway is a technology platform that enables online payments to be made securely between a merchant and a customer. It acts as a secure conduit between the two parties to facilitate the authorization, capture, and settlement of transactions.

Payment Gateway Fees

Payment gateway fees are the costs associated with using a payment gateway, including setup fees, transaction fees, and monthly fees. It is important for merchants to understand the fee structure of their chosen payment gateway to ensure that it is cost-effective for their business.

Payment Gateway Integration

Payment gateway integration is the process of integrating a payment gateway into an e-commerce platform or website. This involves configuring the payment gateway settings, testing payment processing, and ensuring that payment data is handled securely.

Payment Processor

Payment processors are responsible for handling, routing, and processing transactions between the merchant and the payment gateway. They typically work with multiple payment gateways to provide redundancy and ensure that payments are settled quickly and accurately.

Payment Providers

Payment providers are companies that offer a variety of payment services, including payment gateway integration, payment processing, and e-commerce solutions. They often partner with payment gateways to provide a complete payment solution for merchants.

Payment Settlement

Payment settlement is the process of transferring funds from the customer's payment card to the merchant's account after a payment has been authorized. Settlement usually occurs within a few days of the payment being made.

PCI Compliance

PCI compliance refers to the Payment Card Industry Data Security Standard (PCI DSS), which sets requirements for merchants and payment processors to ensure the secure handling of payment card information. Compliance with these standards helps to prevent fraud and protect customer data.

Qualified Security Assessor

A Qualified Security Assessor (QSA) is an independent auditor who is authorized to assess the security of payment systems and certify that they meet the Payment Card Industry Data Security Standard (PCI DSS). When selecting a payment gateway, it is important to ensure that the gateway has been certified by a QSA to ensure that it meets the security standards required for processing sensitive payment information.

Quality of Service

Refers to the level of reliability and security that a payment gateway offers. It is important to select a payment gateway that provides high-quality services to ensure that transactions are securely processed without interruption. Customers expect fast and seamless transactions, so a payment gateway with a track record of reliable service is essential.

Quantity Discounts

Quantity discounts refer to discounts offered to merchants who process a high volume of transactions through a payment gateway. When selecting a payment gateway, it is important to consider whether the gateway offers quantity discounts, as this can help reduce the overall cost of using the service.

Query Parameter

In the context of payment gateways, query parameters refer to the data that is exchanged between the merchant's server and the payment gateway's server. Query parameters can be used to pass information such as transaction amount, currency, and order number. Configuring query parameters correctly is important to ensure that transactions are successfully processed.

Query Retry

Query retry refers to the process of attempting to process a transaction again if the first attempt fails. Payment gateways that offer query retry functionality can help ensure that transactions are processed successfully even if the first attempt was unsuccessful due to a temporary issue such as network congestion.

Queue Management

Queue management refers to the process of managing the flow of transactions through a payment gateway. Payment gateways that offer effective queue management can help ensure that transactions are processed in a timely and efficient manner, minimizing processing delays and reducing the risk of transaction failure.

Quick Checkout

Quick Checkout refers to the process of simplifying checkout to enable customers to complete transactions with minimal effort. Payment gateways that offer a quick checkout feature streamline the checkout flow, allowing customers to complete transactions quickly and efficiently.

Quick Response Code

A Quick Response (QR) code is a square-shaped code that can be scanned using a mobile device to initiate a payment transaction. Payment gateways that offer QR code functionality can help simplify the checkout process for customers by allowing them to simply scan a code to complete a transaction.

Quota

Quota refers to the maximum number of transactions that a payment gateway can process within a specific time frame. When selecting a payment gateway, it is important to consider whether the projected transaction volume will exceed the quota limit, as this may result in processing delays or even failure of transactions.

Quotation

A quotation is a formal estimate of the cost of using a payment gateway's services. Before selecting a payment gateway, it is important to obtain a quotation to assess the cost of using the service, including transaction fees and other charges.

Real-time verification

This refers to a process by which a payment gateway quickly and automatically verifies the accuracy of customer data. Real-time verification helps prevent the submission of incorrect or invalid payment information. Payment gateways may use various methods for real-time verification, such as Address Verification Service (AVS) and card verification codes.

Recurring billing

This refers to the process of charging customers on a regular, recurring basis for products or services. Payment gateways that support recurring billing are ideal for businesses with subscription-based models. The gateway automatically processes payments on a set schedule, reducing manual intervention and minimizing the risk of human error.

Recurring payments

This refers to payments made by a customer on a regular, recurring basis. Examples of recurring payments include subscriptions and installment plans. Payment gateways may offer features for managing recurring payments, such as the ability to automatically charge customers on a set schedule.

Refund

This refers to the return of a portion or the entirety of a payment made by a customer. Payment gateways may require businesses to follow specific procedures for issuing refunds. Refunding payments quickly and efficiently can help maintain customer satisfaction and can protect businesses from chargebacks.

Reserve fund

This refers to a pool of funds held by a payment gateway to cover potential chargebacks and disputes. Payment gateways may require merchants to contribute to the reserve fund by setting aside a percentage of sales revenue. The reserve fund is used to reimburse customers in the event of a chargeback and to cover other related expenses.

Responsive design

This refers to the design of a website or online store that automatically adjusts to the screen size of the device being used to view it. Payment gateways that offer responsive design ensure that the checkout process is easy and intuitive, regardless of whether the customer is using a desktop computer or a mobile device.

Risk analysis

This refers to the process of assessing the risk associated with a transaction. Payment gateways may use various tools, such as machine learning algorithms, to analyze transactions and flag suspicious activity. Risk analysis helps prevent fraudulent transactions from occurring and protects merchants from financial loss.

Risk management

This refers to the measures taken by a payment gateway to mitigate the risk of fraudulent transactions. Payment gateways may use various tools, such as fraud detection algorithms and machine learning, to identify and flag suspicious transactions. Effective risk management can reduce the incidence of chargebacks, protect businesses from financial loss, and maintain customer trust.

Risk score

This refers to the numerical value assigned to a transaction by a payment gateway's risk assessment algorithm. The risk score takes into account a variety of factors, such as the customer's location, transaction history, and the likelihood of fraud. Merchants can use the risk score to determine whether or not to accept a transaction.

Rolling reserve

This refers to a specific type of hold placed on merchant funds by a payment gateway. A rolling reserve is a percentage of a merchant's transaction volume that is held in reserve by the payment gateway for a set period of time. The reserve is meant to serve as a buffer against future chargebacks and disputes. Merchants typically receive their funds after the reserve period has ended.

Sales reporting

This feature allows merchants to track and analyze their sales data, such as number of transactions, revenue, and customer behavior. A good payment gateway should offer detailed reporting to help merchants make informed business decisions and optimize their sales strategies.

Scalability

A payment gateway should be able to handle an increasing volume of transactions as a merchant's business grows. A scalable payment gateway with high reliability and uptime can prevent system overload and ensure seamless transactions for customers.

Security

The level of protection that a payment gateway offers to prevent fraudulent activity or data breaches. A secure payment gateway should have encryption technology and adhere to PCI DSS compliance standards to ensure sensitive information is protected. It should also have fraud prevention measures such as AVS, CVV2, and 3D Secure to authenticate transactions and detect any suspicious activity.

Service fees

Service fees refer to the fees charged by a payment gateway for processing transactions. A good payment gateway should have transparent, competitive rates with no hidden fees, and offer customizable fee structures to suit different business models and transaction volumes.

Settlement and payouts

Settlement refers to the process of transferring funds from a merchant's account to their bank account, while payouts refer to the process of transferring funds to third-party vendors or partners. A reliable payment gateway should offer fast settlement and payout options with transparent fees.

Setup and integration

The process of setting up and integrating a payment gateway onto a website can be complex and time-consuming. A payment gateway that offers easy integration options such as API, plugins, and hosted payment pages can save merchants time and effort.

Simple checkout experience

A complex or confusing checkout process can lead to cart abandonment and loss of sales. A payment gateway with a simple, streamlined, and user-friendly checkout experience can improve conversion rates and enhance customer satisfaction.

Subscription billing

This feature allows merchants to set up recurring payments for subscriptions or services. A good payment gateway should offer flexible subscription options and automated billing to help merchants manage and grow their subscription-based businesses.

Support

Payment gateway issues or errors can disrupt business operations and cause revenue loss. A payment gateway that offers 24/7 customer support via phone, email, or live chat can minimize downtime and provide merchants with peace of mind.

Supported payment methods

A payment gateway should support a range of payment methods such as credit cards, debit cards, e-wallets, and bank transfers. This enables merchants to cater to different customer preferences and expand their customer base.

Tax Compliance

As payment gateway providers process payments on behalf of merchants, they collect and remit sales taxes to state authorities. Merchants should ensure that the payment gateway they select is tax-compliant and provides accurate tax-related data for accounting purposes.

Termination Clause

It refers to the policy that outlines the conditions for terminating or ending the use of a payment gateway. Merchants should look out for termination clauses in their contract because some providers may levy significant charges for early termination. It is essential to evaluate the terms and conditions and opt for providers with fair and reasonable termination clauses.

Third-Party Integrations

Payment gateway solutions should integrate smoothly with various third-party applications such as inventory management, accounting, or e-commerce platforms used by merchants. Integration options available to merchants are critical considerations while selecting a payment gateway.

Time to Settlement

Time between payment confirmation and when the payment appears in a merchant's account is called the settlement period. It affects cash flow and budgeting for businesses. Merchants should verify the time to settlement while selecting a payment gateway because some providers may take longer than others.

Tokenization

It refers to the process of replacing sensitive data like credit card numbers with unique identification symbols or "tokens." Payment gateways use tokenization to protect sensitive information for recurring payments, which does not need to be re-entered by customers, reducing the chances of data breaches or frauds.

Total Cost of Ownership (TCO)

TCO is the total cost that merchants incur when using a payment gateway, including transaction fees, monthly fees, integration costs, and other related costs. Merchants should consider TCO while selecting a payment gateway because the lowest transaction fees do not always mean the most affordable solution.

Transaction Fees

The cost charged by payment gateway providers for each payment processing transaction is referred to as transaction fees. It is an essential factor that merchants consider when selecting a payment gateway. Transaction fees are usually a percentage of the transaction amount along with a flat fee for each transaction. Merchants should compare transaction fees offered by different providers before selecting one that suits their business.

Transaction Limits

Merchants should consider transaction limits offered by payment gateway providers. A maximum transaction value or limit that their gateway can handle may not be enough for some merchants. It is essential to choose a payment gateway that enables them to handle the volume of transactions they expect in the coming months or years.

Trustworthiness

Merchants should consider the credibility, reputation, and industry recognition of payment gateway providers before selecting one. It is critical to choose a provider who is known for secure and reliable payment processing, has excellent customer support, and provides prompt resolutions to any issues. Trustworthiness should be a critical factor while selecting a payment gateway.

Two-Factor Authentication

It is a security process that requires users to provide two methods of authentication, making it challenging for potential fraudsters to breach their accounts. It enhances transaction security measures and creates a safer environment for merchants and customers. Payment gateway solutions that support Two-Factor Authentication (2FA) should be preferred by small and big business alike.

Undisputed Transactions

An undisputed transaction refers to a payment that has been accepted by the customer and cannot be reversed or chargedback. It's important to ensure that payment gateway services are equipped with measures that prevent instances of fraudulent transactions or chargebacks, to reduce the risk of undisputed transactions.

Unit Pricing

Unit pricing refers to the cost of each transaction processed by a payment gateway system. Payment gateway systems with lower unit pricing fees can reduce the overall cost of payment processing for businesses. Before selecting a payment gateway, it's important to compare their unit pricing fees and consider the volume of transactions that the business will process.

Universal Payment Acceptance

Universal payment acceptance refers to a payment gateway's ability to accept and process payments from different payment methods and currencies. A payment gateway that supports a variety of payment methods (such as credit cards, e-wallets, and bank transfers) can expand an online business's customer base and improve sales conversions. When selecting a payment processor, it's important to ensure that it supports a variety of payment methods and currencies.

Upfront Fees

Upfront fees are the costs that a payment gateway charges for services or setup before the transaction even takes place. These fees can include charges for installation, monthly subscription, or gateway service fees. Merchants must factor these fees into the overall cost of using the payment gateway service, and compare them to similar payment gateway providers before making a final decision.

Upgradeability

As a business grows and evolves, it may require additional payment gateway capabilities. Upgradable payment gateway systems allow merchants to add new features or integrate with existing payment systems as their business needs change. It's important to consider the ability to upgrade payment gateway services when selecting a provider to ensure long-term compatibility.

Uptime

Uptime refers to the amount of time that a payment gateway system is operational and available to process transactions. Payment gateway systems with higher uptime rates are more reliable, and reduce the risk of lost sales due to processing errors. When selecting a payment gateway, it's important to check its uptime rate and ensure that the system has measures in place to prevent downtime or data breaches.

Usability

Usability refers to a payment gateway system's user-friendliness and ease of use. A payment gateway that is difficult to use or navigate can discourage customers from making a purchase. Therefore, when selecting a payment gateway, merchants should compare the usability features of different systems and choose one that is easy for their customers to use.

Use Case Scenarios

Use case scenarios refer to common situations in which a payment gateway would be used. Merchants should consider the unique needs of their businesses when selecting a payment gateway, and ensure that it provides the necessary features and capabilities to facilitate their specific use case scenarios. For example, an e-commerce business may require a payment gateway that supports recurring payments, while a brick-and-mortar store may not.

User Interface (UI)

A payment gateway's user interface refers to the layout and design of the payment gateway system. A visually appealing and simple user interface can improve customer satisfaction and boost sales. Merchants should compare the user interface of different payment gateway systems to ensure that customers can easily navigate and understand the payment gateway.

User-Experience (UX)

User experience refers to the overall interaction that a customer has when using a payment gateway system. A payment gateway that is easy to navigate and understand is crucial in order to ensure a smooth transaction process for customers. Frustration with payment gateway systems can lead to abandoned transactions and lost sales. Therefore, it's important to understand the UX features of a payment gateway before selecting one.

VAT (Value Added Tax)

A tax applied to goods and services sold in certain regions, such as the European Union. Payment gateways can automatically calculate and collect the appropriate VAT for merchants.

Vaulting

The process of securely storing customers' payment information for future use. Payment gateways offer this feature to merchants to reduce friction during the checkout process for returning customers.

Velocity

The rate at which transactions are processed by a payment gateway. Merchants must choose a payment gateway with high velocity to ensure that payments are processed quickly and efficiently.

Vendor

The provider of the payment gateway service. Merchants must choose a reputable vendor to ensure reliable payment processing for their customers.

Verification

The process of authenticating the payment information provided by the customer. Payment gateways often employ various methods, such as address verification, card verification value (CVV) checks, and 3-D secure to ensure that the payment information is accurate and valid.

Virtual Terminal

A payment processing tool that enables merchants to input payment information manually. This is typically used for payments made over the phone or by mail.

Visa

One of the major credit card networks that payment gateways can integrate with. Merchants must have a merchant account with a bank to accept Visa payments.

Void

The process of canceling an authorized payment transaction before it is captured. This typically occurs when the customer cancels their order or the merchant determines that the payment is invalid.

Volume Discounts

A pricing model offered by payment gateways that reduces the transaction fees for merchants with a high volume of transactions.

Wallet ID

A Wallet ID is a unique identifier that is used to identify a user's digital wallet. It is required for making payments via digital wallets. Payment gateways that support digital wallets require users to provide their Wallet ID to complete a transaction.

Wallet Pay

Wallet Pay refers to the ability for customers to pay for goods and services via a mobile wallet like Apple Pay, Android Pay, or Samsung Pay. Businesses that offer support for wallet pay offer a convenient alternative to traditional payment methods.

Wallets

A digital wallet is a software application that stores credentials for making online transactions. It allows users to securely store their debit/credit card information, and other related information for making payments. Some payment gateways offer support for multiple digital wallets.

Webhooks

A webhook is a push notification that sends data from one application to another. It is used by payment gateways to send real-time transaction updates to merchants/businesses.

White-label

A white-label solution is a product or service that is developed by one company, but is re-branded and sold by another company under its own name. Some payment gateways offer white-label solutions to businesses who want to re-brand their services.

Winning Bids

Winning bids is a term used in online auctions. When a winner bids on an item and wins the auction, they are required to pay for the item. Payment gateways that support online auctions allow customers to make payments for their winning bids.

Wire Transfer

A wire transfer is an electronic transfer of funds from one bank account to another. Payment gateways that support wire transfers allow businesses to accept payments from customers who prefer to make payments via bank transfers.

Withdrawal

A withdrawal is the process of transferring money from one account to another. Payment gateways that offer support for withdrawals allow businesses to transfer funds to their bank accounts.

WooCommerce

WooCommerce is a plugin for WordPress websites that allows businesses to create and manage an online store. It also provides support for integrating different payment gateways.

Worldpay

Worldpay is a global payment gateway provider that offers a range of solutions to merchants/businesses. Their services include online payments, in-store payments, mobile payments, and more.

www.ingramcontent.com/pod-product-compliance
Lightning Source LLC
Chambersburg PA
CBHW071032220526
45467CB00004B/1623